Praise for
the poetry of
Jeff Mann

Published by Lethe Press
lethepressbooks.com

Cover Design by Ryan Vance
Interior design by Ryan Vance

REDNECK BOUQUET

Gay Poems From Appalachia

JEFF MANN

For Amy Mann, John Ross,
and all my mountain clan.

CONTENTS

Trounced by Princess Puppy: On the Difficulties of Being a Gay Writer in Appalachia

Size queens would agree: the bigger the better. This might be true of the male appendáge, as my husband calls it, but it's not always true of the writerly ego.

All my life I have dreamed of possessing inordinately large self-importance. Indeed, given the proper nourishment, my ego would wax obnoxious, swelling into as bloated a bulk as many I have encountered at writers' conferences and book festivals. However, being both a regional and a gay author makes ego-food hard to come by. Such difficulties have kept my potential arrogance and bad behavior very nicely in check.

As a writer whose work most often focuses on both the gay male and the Appalachian experience, I get an unspoken message from many sources, that my literary labors do not in the long run count. From mainstream editors, publishers, and reviewers. From certain colleagues at Virginia Tech. From urban LGBT folks who regard rustic or regional identity with patronizing contempt. From Appalachian folks who regard gays with pious fear and loathing. Even from certain MFA students, many of whom are fascinated with the urbane and the faddish and have no respect for or interest in artists who speak for subcultures or minorities. To be both queer and regional, these sources tacitly insist, is to be doubly limited in scope, twice as dismissible. LGBT is not universal. Appalachian is not universal. Who, in other words, wants to read about hillbillies and queers? (In order to achieve a more respectable literary reputation, perhaps I should write distanced, obscure lyrics and witty postmodern narratives about heterosexual life in the DC suburbs, but I fear that might require more research than my impatience would permit.)

Many days, these facts make me bitter and disheartened (though the regular consumption of martinis helps lighten my mood). When I brood, I chew over my curmudgeon's litany of disappointments. The public library in my hometown of Hinton, West Virginia, possesses, I am told, of my fourteen books only one. The state newspaper, *The Charleston (WV) Gazette,* entirely ignored my memoir *Loving Mountains, Loving Men,* the first book to deal with gay life in Appalachia. What recognition I've achieved I have scrabbled and fought for, while enviously watching fame come with ease to so many straight folks and city dwellers who successfully network within the literary mainstream. I am often wont to hum, along with Mary Chapin Carpenter, "Everything we got / we got the hard way."

I am not alone in these frustrations, of course. So many of us writers—straight or gay, urban or country—have faced the same tsunamis of indifference and trudged through the same sloughs of self-doubt. We've continued writing as best we can in the face of neglect, obscurity, and the dwindling possibilities of publishing in a world where fewer and fewer people seem to read with any regularity (the seductions of text-messaging, television, and computer games apparently being too powerful to resist). Stubbornness gets us through, sheer orneriness and the inescapable urge to express what we must.

Humor also rescues us. When I want to make laughter out of how unwelcome and invisible I, as a gay author in Appalachia, sometimes feel (like that evil fairy not invited to Sleeping Beauty's christening), I tell the tale of Princess Puppy.

A straight friend of mine, Tiffany Trent—author of several popular young-adult fantasy novels from both Simon and Schuster and Mirrorstone Books—was invited to be part of the Second Annual Author Fair at the Pulaski County Public Library, in the very same Virginia town where my husband and I live. Tiffany encouraged the organizer of the event to invite me, since I've published a goodly number of books and live only a few blocks from the library. The invitation came via e-mail, asking for a description of what I published and a list of my book titles. I responded, honestly and in some detail. I received no reply. When, a few days before the event, I e-mailed the organizer again, she replied by withdrawing the invitation, telling me that the event had too many authors as it was.

Pulaski is, like many small mountain towns, infested with fundamentalist Christians. Was this a case of homophobia? I don't know. I try not to assume the worst, despite my tendency toward paranoia. I do know, thanks to Tiffany's breathless report afterward, that almost all the authors who were celebrated that afternoon were self-published. Tiffany and a poet from Radford University were the only exceptions. The most colorful presence at the author fair was a woman whose make-up rivaled Tammy Faye Bakker's. She chided Tiffany for writing young adult dark fantasy. "Oh dear," she said. "Why can't people stop writing that nonsense and just write wholesome books with good Christian values like mine? You aren't saved, are you?"

Her wholesome Christian books, it turns out, were a series of children's books about Princess Puppy. Best of all, said princess was actually present at the library event. As Tiffany describes it, "a poodle lunged from a cavern of pink tulle piled under a book table. It wore a tutu and tiara and yipped so vociferously that the tiara slid down over its face." Tiffany was later to note, upon closer examination, that the princess was a prince. Yes, here was "a Christian author who turned her dogs into ballet drag queens!"

Tiffany spent the remainder of the event being annoyed by the poodle's manic yapping and listening to a clutch of other authors talk about the importance of letting Jesus into one's life. She was, however, allowed some pleasure as she was packing to leave: "Without warning, the puppy drag princess lifted his leg and pissed all over his pink tulle bed."

Ever since I heard Tiffany's tales of this prissy canine, I've been joking that I need a T-shirt with the slogan "Trounced by Princess Puppy." Part of being marginalized is being excluded—from literary journals, networking opportunities, chances for recognition and publicity—but sometimes being excluded is a blessing. It spares you many an irritation. If I am invited to participate in next year's Pulaski author fair, I think I'll pass.

All that said, snickered, and snarled, there are some sweet advantages to being a gay regionalist who's stubbornly remained on native ground. First of all, filling a literary niche that hasn't been previously occupied is bound to garner at least a little recognition. The fact that no one had ever before published a book about gay life in Appalachia certainly made it easier for me to wrangle a contract out of Ohio University Press for *Loving Mountains, Loving Men*.

My very distinctive literary identity also got me a little attention when a certain much-talked-about film was released soon after *Loving Mountains, Loving Men: The Roanoke Times* christened me "the *Brokeback* Professor." Let's just say that writing about the gay/Appalachian/leather/bear experience might limit my audience, but at least I'm unique.

Second of all, what audience I have wonderfully fuels my determination to keep going. E-mails and letters arrive, infrequently but regularly, thanking me for my publications about gay life in Appalachia. Those who read my work are starved for reflections of themselves and affirmations of their identities. They're most often other gay men from rural backgrounds who don't relate to the urban gay community, with its youth culture, its emphasis on consumerism, sleekness, and refinement. They're pleased to find reading material that reminds them that openly gay and proudly Appalachian are not mutually exclusive states, that one can make a queer life far from gay meccas. Their letters to me are enthusiastic, grateful, and very kind. In moments of my deepest discouragement, their voices remind me that I'm not wasting my time writing about hillbillies and queers.

Responses from thankful readers are not entirely sufficient to quell my complaints. I still make bitter jokes. *When* will my hometown be erecting a statue in my honor? *Why* is my latest poetry reading not crowded with clamoring paparazzi? *Where* is that coterie of young, muscular, goateed groupies to dote on me and offer me their submissive sexual favors? I still quietly envy those writers whose paths have been easier and more conventionally successful. These are the sour feelings of that secretly bulky writer's ego mentioned earlier, one denied the attention it has always believed it deserves.

Still, notes from my readers have led me to a position I never thought I'd inhabit. When I was younger, my father and I used to argue about art. He sided with Tolstoy: the greatest art should contribute to a sense of human unity. I was a firm advocate of aestheticism: beauty first, art-for-art's-sake, and all that. Very Oscar Wilde, very fin de siècle. Since those long-ago arguments, my position has shifted. I'm not suggesting that writers are obligated to produce works that obey Tolstoy's dicta—after all, we write according to our obsessions, not according to literary or aesthetic theory—and I'm still big on beauty, whether it's literary—a well-turned phrase, a memorable metaphor, a moving image--or

4

physical—a mountain range, a snowy pasture, a black beard, a hairy chest. But art that provides not only aesthetic pleasure but also social benefit achieves, it seems to me, the best of both worlds, an amalgam of which both Wilde and Tolstoy might approve.

Being a regional gay writer has limited and marginalized me, I have no doubt. Minority writers rarely have burgeoning majority audiences. The tutu-clad adventures of Princess Puppy, the angst-ridden lives of metropolitan heterosexuals are literary fare more palatable to many than my frank, occasionally erotic, often angry prose and poetry about mountaineer queers. But being doubly marginalized has cultivated a passion in me—much as certain hothouse conditions can force a bulb—for literature that insists not only on beauty but on justice. Frequent frustration such a writing life can be. It is also exhilarating unity—to stand with one's clan, intractable queers past and present—and it is heady privilege—to be part of progress in whatever ways circumstances allow.

ONE

The Gay Redneck Devours
Draper Mercantile

He wakes late, aching for the throb and pound
of a man inside him. Paul Bunyan, perhaps,
striding the snowy cover of the latest Duluth
Trading Company catalog, smiling giant
with a full brown beard, chest bulging
beneath a forester's flannel shirt, Yule tree
hoisted over one huge shoulder.

Hungry, the drive up over Draper Mountain,
past soft siennas of foxtail grass, past breezy
Blow Job Knob where the furtive marrieds
hope and skulk, too horned-up to savor
sprawling vistas of the Alleghenies
and the Blue Ridge. His rusty pickup's blaring
Jason Aldean's new CD of redneck
rock, and what a liner cover, what
a plump and pretty set of lips, the ways

they might be used. Down to Draper, set
among its Valley pastures, where welcome
outside money has saved the Mercantile.
In he lopes, our ridge-runner rump-ranger,
in rural manhood's signifiers: camo pants,
Everlast sweatshirt, Western duster,
cowboy boots, the gray felt hat
bought at a rainy Civil War battle
reenactment, cavalier touch
he likes to think Jeb Stuart would
have worn. Southern small talk with ladies
behind the counter, though the hot lean cook
he's so often admired is nowhere to be seen.
Grilled pimiento cheese, that lunchtime treat
his mother used to make, followed by
blueberry pie and a batch of barbeque
to go. Modal and melancholy, just
the way a weary mountain romantic likes it,

the banjo and the bluegrass. He chews slowly,
trying to savor all—cheese, mayonnaise,
the rich and peppery taste of childhood,
the memoried crust of homemade country sweets
before love fled or bled or was proven
insufficient. What he tries to forget—
how friends and family would feel about how
deeply he longs for a bigger, stronger man
to master him. What he tries to believe,
humming through rapt mouthfuls of Dixie's
caloric comforts—*here in the hills*
I still belong. Here, I'm safe. Here, I'm home.
Here, one day, may all I am be welcome.

Almost Heaven

They're here already, all the elements of paradise. I'm driving
the West Virginia Turnpike, alone in my 4X4, and it's April again,

with Tim McGraw's latest CD and the maples' new green,
redbud shimmering, as if the mountains were spouting

not acid drainage but pink champagne. If sausage biscuits
and my unnatural passion for Krispy Kreme were to stop my heart

right now? Or a drunken trucker, or a rockslide after spring rain,
or a passel of homophobes, or, hell, a meteorite fate has aimed too
        well?

Given the choice, I could drive the Mountain State for eternity,
with a few minor modifications. What's crucial and most salient

about any recipe for heaven? What's left in and what's left out.
No mountaintop removal, no yippy dogs, no badly behaved brats,

no fucking fundamentalists. Only Cabin Creek, running clear
as it was in the Cherokee years. I've got that box of doughnuts,

a bag of my father's sausage/mayonnaise/fresh tomato biscuits,
a cup of coffee, a flask of moonshine, a cooler of beer. The gas

never runs out, sunshine slants and tilts against the wet flex
of thunderstorm. Tim McGraw's here in more than voice,
        grinning,

shirtless. His chest is hairy, sweaty, and in this April light, his skin
seems lightly glazed with gold. I pass him a biscuit, he passes me
        a beer.

Tonight's stop is Helvetia, a big Swiss meal, May apples along the
        creek,
a bed so small ravishing's required. And after that? It's West
        Virginia,

so all delights are here. Tomorrow, perhaps, a campfire on Spruce
Knob,
dawn's surf breaking over Seneca Rocks, a cabin above the
Bluestone River

in October's sugar maple burn. Tim first, then Eric Bana, then
Gerard Butler,
then every other man I have ever hankered for and been denied,

and then my patient partner John, with two cats and a farmhouse,
isolated,
sprawling, in the Potomac Highlands. Heaven's only Appalachia
perfected.

Heaven's a pickup truck and two men together, in cowboy hats
and boots,
singing endlessness along mountain backroads. We're hitting St.
Albans'

Red Line Diner for hot dogs and fries, rocking in starlight over
Lost River.
We're swimming in the simmering New, liquid jade below
Sandstone Falls,

making love along the Greenbrier, beneath sarvisberry and
redbud bloom,
in this year's bluebells and bloodroot, last year's humus and fallen
leaves.

Yellow-Eye Beans

I sort them as I was taught
(is this the way the Norns
allot destinies?) picking out
gravel, bits of dirt,
the shriveled, discolored ones
not fit to eat, fated for
the trash. Sort, rinse, soak
overnight, season with
onion, hog jowl, bacon grease.
Some more objective
observer might see in
my kitchen gestures—sorting
these yellow-eye beans, or
stringing half-runners, or
rolling out pie crust or biscuits—
my father's, and, behind those,
his mother's, yours. Hillfolk
head for beans and cornbread
when the world turns surly—
pinto, yellow-eye, October.
These were your favorite.
Simmering them, I remember you.

Nanny, what would you think
of me now, twenty years after
your death, with my bushy
grizzly-bear beard, my myriad
tattoos, my lust for chest hair,
the man I live with? My guess
would be, after a short lecture
on the Bible, a book I never
much cared about to begin with,
you'd settle down to table
with us, admiring how
handsome this home is
John's made for me. I've
learned a lot in twenty years,

and at last it would be my turn
to cook for you. I promise
you'd be proud
of how well the beans
and cornbread came out
(and if you like this meal,
y'ought to taste
my buttermilk biscuits). But
before we ate, I'd invite
you to say what grace
you wanted in this queer
and pagan home, and so you
would, words brief and deep,
Pass the chowchow
following closely on *Amen.*

Green Man
(for John)

The gifts you leave in my desk's bud vase vary—
a white rose, a sprig of rosemary, grape hyacinth
or species tulip. All summer you have labored,
and now, mid-August, the house is surrounded

with acanthus and honeysuckle, coneflower
and black-eyed Susan, geraniums, hostas,
julep mint. In the tiny garden, squash vines
refine their gold. In the fig tree, plump fruits ripen.

If I am the Lord of the Animals—their furry rut,
their hard-horned musk—vacillating wildly
between nuzzling affections and growling ferocity,

you are the Lord of the Greenwood, forest foliage
twining from your beard and callused fingertips,
swathing me in fertile and protective shade.

Dear Pastor Dickweed,

Yesterday my New Orleans buddy Neil came to visit me,
in this small conservative mountain town you and I share.
Not a mile from your Prayer Infirmary, from your precious
Sunday congregation, your indoctrinated brats, I stripped
Neil down and tied his hands behind his back, here in
my curtained living room, after good red wine and barbeque.
Were you reading the Old Testament as I spoon-fed him
homemade cheesecake ice cream, dribbled it here and there,
licked it off his chin, his big soft nipples, his belly hair, as
he grinned—what a stunning smile—and nuzzled it off
my torso, as we swapped cream from bearded mouth
to mouth? This morning, sweet souvenir, my chest hair
and goatee are still sticky-stiff. Dear Pastor Dickweed,
were you railing against morphodites, their hellish crusade,
when I knotted a camo bandana between Neil's white teeth,
led him upstairs by his cock, pushed him belly-down
on the bed, ate his ass, his beautifully furry ass, for
nigh onto an hour? Jerry Falwell is dead, Dickweed,
your vast book's the gilded guts of pulpwood trees.
Neil's butt-fur was a mythic forest, his hole a Viking
mead-cup. When he came, I rubbed his nectar into
my belly hair, into my beard. Bear Heaven would be
keeping him bound forever beside me, riding him
into the stars, never saying goodbye. You are looking
for God in the wrong direction, purblind Dickweed.
Follow my lead: earth's the place to start, not sky.

The Misanthrope Stands Amid Stumps

Stump-scars,
to be more precise, for even
the stumps are gone, leaving this array
of dirt-mounds where hundred-year-old trees used to be.

Someone
should be horsewhipped.
Last fall, on the way to class, I strode
past them. Species didn't matter—maple, oak,

Bradford pear—
only the great fiery aureole
each evoked, the gold-leaf of cat's eye,
Byzantine saviors scattering benedictions.

I leant palm
or cheek against their barks,
their great peristyle pulsing with
the planet's heartbeat, company so much finer

than most
of my whining plebeian race.
"Imagine," say the chain saws, the office-
suited powers behind their sawdust-spraying teeth,

"Imagine
the buildings to come!
More people! More computers!
A space-age overhead causeway, arcing like a rainbow

of technology!
Give us use, not aesthetics.
Trees are weeds where they are not wanted.
Haul them off!" A little less green-gold this April,

a little less
soughing jade in June,
leaves shivering like lovers
beneath the wind's fond tickle, the gray rain's soft

or violent griefs.
Soon enough, raucous
bulldozers, concrete, heaps of mud.
The common call this progress, with rusty knives

deepening
a wound. I say
it is humans we can spare,
not trees. For those who measure beauty

in board-feet,
let them count their earnings
chained to limbs they amputated,
burnt to husks of bone amidst the heaped

leavings of trees
they felled. Reeks and howlings
rising to heaven, a great helix of smoke.
Between my fingers, I sift the rich ash. Fine food for saplings.

Huntington Lane

It is always summer there, always 1991.
Oak leaves are thick and glossy, you are
forever 32 and in love. His townhouse
is shadowy and cool. You savor time
together before his husband comes home.
My lover, you whisper to yourself, incredulous,
my lover. Your lover brews coffee, talks sex
magick, shows you how his basil plants
are coming along. He hasn't shaved or bathed
today, just for you, knowing how you love
his armpits' aroma in your beard, rough
grit of cheek stubble against your lips.
You suspect, though you do not yet
know, this passion is grander than any
you will ever taste again, and when
he and husband leave at summer's end,
you will spend the next twenty years
driving past that street sign, never
turning onto Huntington Lane (What was
the town house number? You cannot
remember.), that street where oak leaves
never browned, your deepest depths
were sounded, where black-bearded youth
awaits you still among the deathless basil.

The Gay Redneck Visits Heavener Hardware

The contrast between inner and outer
layers pretty much sums this day up.
Beneath the bland cream-colored
turtleneck sweater, his blue T-shirt,
carefully concealed from public view,
says *Butch Bear—Beefy, Brawny,*
Hungry, Horny, Stocky, Hairy,
Manly, Sweaty. Our scruffy
mountaineer, in a luminous
masochist mood, strides down
the hardware aisles with jaunty
step, more than eager for tonight:
Master JW, his favorite Roanoke
sadist Top, the paddling bench
and St. Andrew's cross that await
roped-down struggles, groans
well stifled by a pair of dirty briefs.
"Finally covering that woodpile?"
says the tall, good-looking, built
and bearded—which is to say
totally fuckable—clerk behind
the counter. "Yep. Finally,"
says our grinning redneck, pulling
out his credit card. The tarp's
wide and thick, just the thing
to protect the carpet at three a.m.,
when, mummified from neck
to ankle in Saran-Wrap and duct
tape—Christ's cerecloth cocoon—
he's basting in rapture and his
own streaming sweat, sprawled
upon a tarp-caught, fragrant
piss-puddle his flesh distilled
from thirstily swilled cheap red wine.

My Sister's Potato Salad
(for Amy)

Just another mounting midlife crisis,
this anticlimax, this blasphemer's weed
thorn-brake of complaints.

My job's half-pointless, powerless,
my salary's pathetic, flea-food,
my apartment's a fusty pigeonhole.

Dreams of fame decompose
like toadstools, puddles
of reeking ink,

and no one around is worth the ardor.
Yes, my only PhD's
in Dissatisfaction.

Still, here I am, sitting in
this sunny Summers County kitchen,
spooning up a bowl

of your fresh potato salad.
Our grandmother would be proud.
Just the right mayonnaise/mustard balance,

a few sliced green peppers,
celery's crunch, a few pinches of oregano.
For five minutes, I am completely happy.

Krispy Kreme Fantasia

I want to imagine it again, from this distance. November dawn in the Kanawha Valley, sunny, hungry. The morning after watching *A Walk on the Moon* and falling in love with Viggo Mortensen yet again, here I am in South Charleston's Krispy Kreme, savoring a few of that day's featured doughnuts, pumpkin spice cake, when Viggo strides in—slant of miracle, hymn of sunlight—lost in the mountains, in need of a friend, craving sweets, hot coffee, a warm bed, his married past and parenthood forgotten for the nonce.

Reader, I took him home. I pulled off his duster, flannel shirt, wife beater, faded jeans and cowboy boots. I spent the weekend loving his lean and honey-hairy chest, his ass pale as Icelandic skies or the heart of a McIntosh apple, sweet as doughnut icing to several senses. (Watch the film again to savor these details). I bound him tightly to the bed and kept him for days, detaining God's gifts as best I could, and everything was heady with his submission.

My nakedness lies atop his still, my lips bless his brow even now, here in words warming one empty, unexceptional morning, fantasy edging this aging day, details of the impossible, the alternative.

Country Kids

Other than those students courageously,
openly queer, they are my favorites,
the country kids. They hail from Wytheville
and West Virginia, Woodstock, Southside,
the Blue Ridge, the Shenandoah, the hills
of Craig, Pulaski, Botetourt and Giles,
with their muddy cowboy boots, chunky
belt buckles, trucker caps, blessedly
impeccable manners, Southern vowels
slow and broad as mine, boys with
their bushy-handsome goatees, girls
with their big hair and tight jeans, telling
tales of four-wheeling and deer-hunting,
the time some well-off snot from the DC
suburbs made fun of their local accents,
called them ridge-runner or hillbilly.
I am less than the slick, urbane professor
they might expect (loafers, ties, corduroys?)
with my own camo baseball caps, cowboy
duster, scuffed boots and Rebel beard, eager
passions for Southern food and pickup trucks.
I am more than the mountain man I appear,
joking about my lust for country-music star
Tim McGraw, mentioning my husband
of many years, explaining what the bear-paw
and Lambda tattooed into my left biceps signify.
Southern Baptist and right-wing Republican
many of them might be, yet we feel so much
at home together that they bring me ramps
and deer jerky, creecy greens, kudzu jelly,
raspberry moonshine, all the rural delicacies
that delight the redneck heart, gifts of
a shared and honest fondness that might
turn toward change, quietly political.

Country Kitchen—
Christiansburg, Virginia

Sweet iced tea with lemon, yes.
Country-fried steak with peppered
milk gravy, yes. Fried okra with Tabasco,
buttered limas, butterscotch meringue pie,
yes, yes, yes, praise the Lord, yes.
The waitress and I share the same
vowels, the same mountain cadence
and lilt. "Thanks very much, ma'am.
This looks great!" "You're welcome,
honey. Here's more tea. Y'all enjoy."

I had a lover's quarrel with the world,
said Robert Frost. I the same,
though more specifically with
my native region. And Lord God,
how I love you, my sweet Southland.
Let me today forget your toadish
preachers, your devout Republican
majority, your swinish family values,
your vicious crusades against
same-sex marriage, how you refuse
to love your queer children back.
Let me fill my mouth with the tastes
of home, share bites with my Yankee
husband. I belong here, though

you will not believe it. Outside,
among November's blowing leaves,
my pickup truck cools among all
the other four-by-fours. Picture-
framed over our table, my hero Lee
rides, victorious at Chancellorsville.
The restaurant radio's playing my
Nashville favorites: Luke Bryan,
Chris Young, Kathy Mattea, Tim McGraw.
In the far corner sits a black-goateed,

burly country boy in cowboy boots,
Mountaineers baseball cap, and camo
pants, younger version of myself
whom I would gladly woo and ravish.

Appalachia, I want no other place:
no traffic-snarly gay ghetto, no over-
priced noise-wormy urban warren.
Beloved Baptist-blighted hills, can't
we forget the other's supposed sins
for an hour? Put down your vengeful
cross, and I'll sheath my flaming sword.
Let's avoid religion or politics, speak instead
about the crown of frost on Draper's Mountain,
the silver fog of meadow milkweeds,
the persistent green of autumn kale,
what brands of livestock feed are on sale
at the nearest Tractor Supply Company.
Once my butterscotch pie is done, then

truck out the woe of Leviticus, cast out
the unrighteous and the wild, and once
more I'll be the godless freak and you
again will be my batshit-crazy mad-dog foe.

The Mountaineer Queer, Diagnosed as Dying, Runs Amok

Week 1: Get started while still strong. Plot logistics, fetch supplies.
Lowe's: rope, chain, padlocks, duct tape. Mr. S Leather:
ball-gag, bit-gag, blindfold, handcuffs, paddle, flogger.
Kroger: condoms, lube. Firing range: hone skills.

Week 2: Stalk/chloroform/kidnap Tim McGraw. Cover tracks!
Carry off to remote mtn. cabin/love nest.

Weeks 2-3: Use Tim thoroughly/gently/frequently. Men, like
stallions, need broken in. Feed well. Cuddle and coddle.
Dote, adore. (Paddle/flog resistance.)

Menu for a Well-Behaved Captive: Lots of Dickel
(mint julep? Sazerac?). Fancy cheeses—Humboldt
Fog? Camembert? Cambozola? Champignon? Dinner:
barbequed ribs, cole slaw, cornbread, collards.
Dessert? Pie! Coconut cream. Shoo-fly. Pecan.
Breakfast? Krispy Kreme doughnuts! Sausage biscuits!
(Fuck the calories, man. You're dying.)

Weeks 4-40: Continue passionate use, increasingly vigorous.
Savor, savor. 39 weeks together hardly sufficient,
despite looming deadline. Buy cream of coconut,
wildflower honey: best lapped off body hair. Vary menu
to keep captive happy: fried chicken, pasta carbonara,
rinderrouladen, eggplant Parmesan, cheese enchiladas,
moussaka, Cajun bread pudding/rum sauce, Key lime pie.

Last Night Together: Split bottle of champagne. Demand
performance: "Please Remember Me"/"Live Like You
Were Dying" (accompany on guitar). Release in vicinity
of Nashville. (Tuck apology to wife in underwear.)

Weeks 41-43: Take advantage of Nashville location. *Carpe diem*!
More hot country music stars! Abduct/savor/ravish/
release Chris Cagle. Hone skills at firing range.

Weeks 44-45: Abduct/savor/ravish/release Jason Aldean. Firing range.

Week 46: Abduct/savor/ravish/release Zac Brown. Firing range.

Week 47: Abduct/savor/ravish/release Chris Young. Firing range.

Week 48: Abduct/savor/ravish/release Toby Keith. Keep mouth
taped at all times. Goddamn conservative! Heavy flogging
required. Firing range.

Week 49: Regretfully relinquish love. Buy guns, ammo, whetstone.
Sharpen knives/swords. Firing range.

Week 50: Execute plague of crazy fuckers, i.e., prominent
Republicans, Christian fundamentalists. Cf. Southern
phrase: "They *needed* killin."

Week 51: Execute more of same. Plentiful as roaches/fleas/earthworms!

Week 52: Execute more of same. Save Confederate Bowie knife for
most loathsome.

Last Day: Feel heroic/mythic. Snarf final Krispy Kreme. Leave suicide
note (in blank verse), journal (for historians), money (for
cremation/black granite obelisk). Before law arrives, off
self in Byronic manner. Mtn.top during thunderstorm!
Brandish Viking sword; pray for lightning. Use prosaic
pistol/leave unseemly mess if weather proves disobliging.

The Gay Redneck Invites
City Sappho for a Rural Visit

I know you're hesitant. Why would any queer
visit here, the land of conservative and devout
normality? Much less buy a home? And, after
nearly thirty years, you know better than many
I'm freakier than most. There's the bag of leather
toys in the upstairs closet, a heap of bondage videos,
pagan statues on the mantelpiece—Cernunnos
and Cerridwen, Pan, Bast, Lilith, Thor.
There's a kilt in the closet carefully mothballed,
two swords and a scimitar mounted on the wall,
Tim McGraw calendar in the breakfast nook.

No, none of us is simple. Some part of you
suspects, I suspect, that I am mad not to leave
my mountains, flee to Dupont Circle, the Castro,
as if academic peanuts might allow that. Well,
hell, a beard and cowboy boots get a guy far
in this town, especially if you can slop the sugar
of Southern charm, and I can. It's what the Viceroy
does, or those moths in northern England—
natural selection turned them dun to match
industrial smoke. You should see how the sour
woman at the city office country-smiles when I
show up to pay my water bill wearing a cowboy hat.
She probably listens to Tim McGraw and Chris Cagle
as much as I do, though I can't imagine she wants
to ravish them half as much.

                              Listen, I promise,
if you come down, we don't even have to leave
the house. John and I will get slurry on martinis,
and you can drink that nasty hop-juice Bud Light
(Tim's favorite beer—that boy needs a Daddy
to teach him the finer things). I'll even make
your favorite, eggplant Parmesan, and we'll
whine about the calories later. Come in winter,

and we'll have a fire. If you feel exploracious,
we can always infiltrate the local Christian
bookstore, since I know you're writing lately
on those motherfuckers, the Religious Right,
of which we have 'round hyer, as you might
guess, a poisonous plentitude. There's even
a Prayer Infirmary,whatever the hell that is,
just over the hill. They would be the reason
to immigrate, those pious fools, ubiquitous,
on whom I ache to whet my thirsty swords
(odd for a lawyer's son to so resent the law).

But this morning I walked to the farmer's market,
past an arch of morning glories as blue as
my Nanny's trellis two decades back. I bought
green beans, squash, red bell peppers for
next to nothing, hankered for the fried pies,
the homemade bread (what my buddy calls,
in longing, carbolicious; is every queer
counting carbs?). Everyone was friendly,
for a few seconds I felt I belonged (isn't that
part of Maslow's pyramid?), for sometimes
simple surface means a lot. I was just another
local in tattered wife beater, camouflage
shorts, silver-streaked beard stubble,
Pulaski Blue Jays baseball cap. No matter
I'm a cock-sucker, ass-fucker, aficionado
of ropes and gags. I belong here as much
as any of them, among what sprouts and leafs,
among black walnuts edging my walk home,
the virgin's bower, its feathery whirls of seeds
that spread like midlife after perfume
and the flower, and mallards floating down
Peak Creek, along another inescapable
autumn, natives balanced between
our mountain water, our mountain sky.

TWO

The Gay Redneck Rationalizes Pie Day

First, because he needs a break from the low-carb diet:
    the damned eggs and bacon, eggs and bacon;
    the lean cuts of meat, meat, meat;
    the Virginia Quickstep courtesy of Splenda;
    the cruel absence of pasta, corn, and buttermilk biscuits.

Second, because he can't punish fundamentalists:
    punch the pious pamphlet-toting pricks
        who come to the door with witnessing
        in mind;
    take a sword to the Republican politician
        who wants to return anti-sodomy
        statutes to the state's legal code;
    aim a bazooka at all those churches
        whose members voted to outlaw
        same-sex marriage in Virginia.

Third, because onanism is the only option
    in a mountain town so small:
    he can't grope the chunky-assed, blond-bearded
        Food City clerk;
    can't court the no-doubt-straight dark-goateed
        and tattooed Tractor Supply employee;
    can't abduct and ravish Jessy Ares and Hunter Marx,
        Heath Jordan and Trent Locke,
        RJ Danvers and Damien Crosse,
        the DVD gods of his gay porn universe.

Every Friday's Pie Day at the Draper Mercantile.
Excitedly, he ogles the options:
    blueberry, pecan, coconut cream, butterscotch,
    Dutch apple, lemon chess, strawberry/rhubarb.
He settles on the coconut. Master of sublimation,
    for a few minutes lord of sugar's accessible heaven,
he takes his time, as he would riding a man—
    savoring each bite, sweet distraction
    from hate, creamy substitute for ardor.

Storm Windows

Dear God, I scribble—writing's
the only legal response left—
the boy who just put in new storm
windows on the second floor. Smaller,
younger version of Tim McGraw.
About five foot ten, mid-twenties,
very handsome, dark-goateed face,
fine physique, sweatshirt pulling
up outside the office window as
he stretched up to affix the glass,
revealing a line of belly hair, Jesus,
Apollo's lyre. Crazy-agitated
while he was here, couldn't get enough
furtive peeks, relieved and aching when
he and his buddies left. Just the kind
to bring out the Top in me. Damn,
my page groans, and again desire
fated to die unsated rewrites
disobliging reality, veering into
fantasy: *to see him bare-chested,*
hands bound behind his back, tight
ropes creasing his torso, mouth taped
shut, pants around his ankles, as I
make a feast of his hairy ass, open him
up for a long plowing. Kidnap, rape,

storm windows. What's the metaphor
here? It's mid-December. Soon, for some,
the days will lengthen. Wind was cold
about him, about the precarious height
he worked. He's twenty years younger,
and with those looks has to have a girl
somewhere, no doubt perfumed, painted,
blonde. Lust and awe, no action
verbs allowed but negatives. I did not
slip my hands beneath his sweatshirt
to gauge his chest hair's rich extent.

I did not say, "Stay. I'll keep you warm."
Oh, it's the same old storm, no sealed-up
shelter made by man ever proof
against it, it's another hopeless
longing slurred into syllables for want
of more intimate outlet. I'm paying
for new storm windows to keep
the heat in, the cold out. Beauty
today installs the opposite: his skin,
imaginary, warm, remote, emphasizes
the chill inside this house, the pane
fate firmly inserts between us.
This goateed redneck boy's only
an image behind a clear hard
sheet of glass I touch. Atop his face
glimmers my own, silvery evidence
of another man's unremarkable mid-
life: pathetic, foiled, an obstinate fire.

Daddy's Cabbage

The huge head of cabbage fills his lap,
milky jade moon,
still a little grimy from the gardens at Forest Hill. As if
he'd unearthed a dinosaur egg,
or caught a minor asteroid on the fly. His smile is broad,
proud, and in his face
even at age eighty, there's the force of Palatinate farmers,
founders of our bloodline,
men little different from us, despite the centuries, loving
hearth fire, Moselle,
sauerkraut flavored with bacon grease, a beautiful body
       undressed.

What will Daddy do
with cabbage? (In West Virginia, we squander nothing. We use,
as he likes to say,
every part of the pig except the squeal, so
you can be sure that,
short of three or four outer leaves peeled off
for the compost pile,
nothing will be wasted). He'll cook cabbage rolls, perhaps,
the recipe his mother learned
in the 1920s off an immigrant from Hungary.
Or fried cabbage,
that New Year's tradition, cooked with a coin
for luck to come.
Or chow chow, the homemade relish we spoon
atop brown beans
to satisfy our taste for sweet/sour, that German yearning.

Whatever form it takes,
we are expected to make a fuss, my sister and I, expatiate on
the high deliciousness
of cabbage, as his ego demands. Satellites all our lives, we're
       unable
to imagine this customary
orbit suddenly without a center, when the hill will open

and ancestors stream out
to take him in, leaving us with only cans of chow chow
and his last summer's
cabbage heads stored in the pantry. It is, perhaps, the nearness of
     this future

that permits me finally to admit—
at age forty-four, despite legacies of neurosis and the usual
filial resentments—
that I love my father. To the photograph I whisper the secret.
The farmer smiles back, gray-browed
Depression child, self-reliant, triumphant. *Trust no one*, he seems
     to say.
We grew this,
the earth and I. You must learn to live without needing the world.

Mike

In the house, in the railroad/river town,
in the mountains I think of as home, my mother's
dusting somewhere, my father's busy sweeping
storm-strewn pine straw off the front lawn,
and I'm sliding barbequed country-style ribs
into the oven but fretting about the carbs
in the sauce when there's a knock on the front
door. To my stunned surprise, Mike, it's you,
my black-bearded high school hunting and
drinking buddy, flashing me your glorious
catfish grin. "Good God, you haven't aged
at all, " I drawl, amazed by your handsome looks.
Stepping out onto the porch, I find myself
surprisingly seventeen. You reach up (and how
I love how much smaller you are than I),
embrace me, and begin kissing me, insistently,
passionately, while fumbling with my clothes.
Soon we're both naked, on the floor of the porch.
You're on top of me, kissing me, kissing me.
I run my hands over your muscled back—spring-
smooth skin, scarred here and there with war
wounds—then kiss your hairy chest, tongue
your nipples, crane my head to get a better look
at the tight, pale curves of your ass. My mother
peers through the screen. My father passes us
as, chores done, he enters the house. I muster
an apologetic gesture and a sheepish smile, as if
to say, "Sorry! He's all over me! What can I do?"
then run my hand over your butt-cheeks. When
I express surprise at your man-on-man fervor,
you explain that a solicitous football coach
had converted you to the well-lubed raptures
of consensual sodomy. I'm gripping your hips,
praising such a generous cosmos, and you're
lubing us up, raging-eager to sit on my prick
when I awake—the dawn-manic tabbies must
have knocked something over—fifty-four again,

flooded with wonder and a great gratitude,
that erratic chemistries of dream had given me
that brave, beautiful country boy I'd always
wanted to hold, still young, still young, still young,
Mike naked, hairy, and submissive in my arms.

The Old Lecher Regretfully Dismisses Narcissus

How many years have I loved you? Well, not loved,
that's part of the problem. Desired. Desired.
I well recall that boy you used to be,
with shaggy black hair and full black beard,
thick dark coating his legs, black fur rimming
his nipples, feathering finely over his belly, over
his chest. Yardstick out, he's measuring his own
cock and sighing smugly, staring into the mirror,
murmuring, "Hell, yes! Not bad! I'd fuck that!"
That blessed ascent lasted for decades: furrier,
stronger, more of the manly flex and swagger,
unkempt mountain boy become the rampant
Daddybear, bald, tattooed, ferocious,
redneck beard-bush streaked with gray, pecs
and arms dense with free-weights muscle, just
the stud to wield a crop or porno-paddle.
Thirty years, burly Narcissus, loving
your reflection. The hill drops off here,
in your fifties, where the bags beneath your eyes
have the heft and hue of rainclouds, the hair
upon your breast is less black than silver,
where erections thrust and flag like autumn squalls.
No diet seems sufficient to banish your belly-bulge,
and the fine black fur of which you were so proud
evaporates in patches from your shins and thighs.
I feel not love for you, sadly, but pity, pity
for you and for all the silvery survivors. Certainly
not desire. Perhaps you need liposuction,
a dye job, a testosterone patch? A time
machine? The hot, sweet men now worth my lust
are decades younger, and you, I'm sad to say,
my grizzled twin, are now too old to want.

The Misanthrope Visits
Eggleston, Virginia

Few outside the Virginias know her story,
so briefly I tell it here: Mary Draper Ingles,
captured by the Shawnee in 1755. In Big Bone,
Kentucky, she escaped and made her way home—
four hundred and fifty miles along the Ohio,
the Kanawha, the New River. Here at Eggleston,
she scaled these palisade cliffs, her last great obstacle.
Found by hunters, nourished with broth,
she was at last reunited with her husband.

I've heard this tale since grade school,
in several courses I teach it now,
yet today, staring up at that palisade precipice
she mounted, I wonder briefly what she would do,
reaching the top of this Pan's pipe of stone, looking
down not on her century but mine.

Today the Eggleston Springs Camper Park
is set beside the New River's jade-green flow.
Dozens of aluminum trailers, fisherman's hovels,
junk cars hunch amidst dust and weeds.
Paper cups and beer cans scatter the ditches, fishing line
tangles the sycamore leaves, plastic this-and-that
embeds riverbank mud. Everyone wants
a little taste of woods and water, a little rural room.

I see her on the cliff-top, rag-clad, bloodied, skeletal-
starved. I beg her to go back, but on she comes,
lowering her bare feet from rock to rock,
crying for her husband, leaving the wilderness behind.

Joe-Pye Weed

Old rose courier of decay,
I join the first cold night-rains driving

the windows down, the wind-wake
bustle of redtop grass introducing

autumn along interstate medians
across Appalachia. A small

purple spot stains the sole
of the foot, silver moss spreads

across the temple's black. I am the heart's
arhythmia, standing dizzy in the shower,

yellow jackets in their obsessive concentrics
about orchard windfalls. I am the sawdust

clue the termite leaves, someone else's
scent in your lover's moustache.

Crickets

Unnoticed all summer, by the first week of fall
they've become our insomnia. Popping under
the laundry hamper, clicking through the dying
dust-mop zinnias and parched borders of alyssum—
even our stale quilts echo with their ebony
fiddles of desperation. The ditches chill
with melancholy and redtop grass, the wild grapes
ripen, by the end of October crickets will
have filled the foundations of the house.

In the Church of the Pilgrims, dying mimosa light.
The mouths of all the handsome brim over
with elegies. The aisles end in feather masks,
paintings, poems, cremains. We spill from the maw
of the memorial service, blinking back salt and mourning
ourselves, turning our faces to the scalpel
of the spire as it stabs a streakless vacuity
of chicory-blue, counting the numbers we have loved.

We go home separately but dream the same dream:
our beds fill with burning leaves, oases clog
with animal bones. We eat mistletoe berries
off a communion platter, webs mist over
our perfect muscles, temples smoke over
with ruin, the black panic of crickets
chirring retreat before premature frost.

A Brief Christian Visit; Or, the Butch Bottom Sends Old Ladies Packing
(for JW and Geri)

In the face of such talcum-dusted aggression,
it's taken me decades to become this blunt.
"Is this a Christian visit?" I ask the two old ladies
standing on my stoop with Bibles clutched like
sinister infants in their arms. "I'm sorry, ma'am,"
(that intro being what's left of Southern manners)
"but I'm a homosexual and a pagan and I really want
nothing to do with Christianity." They look up at
the man I've become, my bulky, muscled frame,
my smooth-shaved head and camo cargo shorts,
my bearded frown. How much do they see, how
much do they comprehend? My left arm's entirely
ink-sleeved: C.S.A., a Mars symbol, a pentagram,
the face of the Horned God, a bear paw, thorns
and thistles, a flaming sword. From the sides
of my wife beater spill chest hair and the purple
bruises of a damned fine pec caning to match
the flogging welts across my back. Really,
whose world do they think this is? Off they go,
scuttling down the front walk, past the flower
beds brimful of poppies and peonies my handsome
husbear's planted. Sweet, silvery ladies, wives
of a long dead god, my body will do what it pleases.

Here's to Fucking the Famous

Tim McGraw with his hands tied behind his back
and his legs in the air. Chris Cagle stripped shirtless
and barefoot, briefs taped in his goateed mouth,
roped to a chair. Toby Keith strung from the rafters,
redneck ass reddened with a belt. Gerard Butler spread-
eagled on the bed, black bearded, ball-gagged and drooling,
sweat dewing his chest pelt. Keith Urban pale and naked,
cuffed to a gurney, both ends filled, mumbling for help.
Fifty approaches, and fat, staid celibacies of marriage.
February gray, yet here come snowdrops and hyacinths,
the nestling love of the tabby cat. These fantasies are simply
what Hardy spoke of, throbbings of noontime at eve,
liquid ways of filling CVs, the laptop's snow screen.
Join bound captives in their grunting, in Kleenex come clean.

Rainbow Chard, Bear Bouquet

For Valentine's Day, my husbear brings me not
stiff and scentless out-of-season roses
in their white cardboard coffins, or sad cyclamen
fated to shrivel like my root-bound youth,

not garish candy hearts or oversweet
chocolates, but *skyr*, beef filets, oysters, and this
huge bouquet of chard: orange, red,
and purple stems, the leaves like elephant ears,

glossy green flags, leather wings
scalloped at the edges. We are, I fear, well past
the highest hopes, the largest luminosities, but here

are fire-flicker and Clos du Bois, snow's
feet heaped outside, carpetbagger steak,
the lemony, spicy savor of wilted rainbows.

Harland Sanders Café and Museum

All the stories, incalculable as new-green
leaves burgeoning this Kentucky spring

while the past grades down to humus. Here,
for 26 years, a man sold gas along Route 25,

mixed spices for fried chicken batter, and the tourists
flowed through, the tourists fed, and now I

am part of it, I superimpose myself, viewing
the replicas of the 30s dining room and kitchen,

sitting by a life-sized model of the Colonel
and grinning for a Facebook photograph.

My brief history here is entirely transfixed
by a hot redneck boy in his twenties whom I study

over my husband's shoulder. Solemn green eyes,
brown beard, spiky tattoos revealed by

short T-shirt sleeves, and his right arm
in a sling. I have a leg; John has a thigh.

"Best biscuit I've ever had in a restaurant," I growl,
licking my lips. "He's disabled," jokes John,

"I'll bet we can take him." "Oh, for a sweet breast
of white meat," I sigh, watching my prey leave

with a gaggle of older female kin. At age 53,
I regard with both regret and relief

the approaching day when I might choose a biscuit
over a boy's bare buttocks, though my guess is that

death might precede such an abdication.

The Gay Redneck, Aging

cusses the mirror, plucking silver from his eyebrows
  popping glucosamine pills

thanks God for those precious rarities
  hot young men with Daddy fetishes

brushes dust from his cowboy hats

buys arch support for his cowboy boots
  back support for his rusty
    Toyota truck seat

Buzzard

Ingrate.
          Look at me.
                    Stop your stupid
          shudder and shout.
I am not death
          but what redeems
                    rot, what saves us all
          from waste.
This is the miracle
          each clean skull
                    shall praise, how
          I consume the reek,
carbon's sad,
          entropic fate, the oozy
                    loss of lovers and kin,
          and make of agony
and absence
          this red hook
                    tearing torsos,
          these dark feathers
riding the currents
          of a great breath,
                    folding twilight
          over the carcass
of the sun.

Pressure-Washer Prayer

It must be like this on the river's
far side, the first minutes without
heartbeat or breath, death's
pressurized scalpel peeling clean
the sour soul—just as this lance
of water skims from the back deck's
surface decades of greenish scum, color
of murk under evergreens, smelly
cataracts of algae sealing the sight
of ponds. What's left is the bright grain
of origin, the fresh and resurrected
wood. Blast it off, Lord, how much I hate
the hateful world, whittle away
the coarse-bitter bark slabbing over
hope and any capacity for delight.
Hack off the Republicans, rap's stereo-
throb, screaming babies, barking dogs.
Slash away the vicious Christians,
the fungoid politicians they breed,
the massacres of mountains and streams.
Blast off lesser men's undeserved blessings,
kin's vampiric selfishness, passion's
slow recession, the myriad weaknesses
rooted in this stuttering self. Excoriate
the lesions left by beautiful boys I cannot
possess, swinish enemies I cannot throttle
blue. Let light and water leave me tattered,
breathless, simple, strong, and clean. I
will be gods' bone, face and name long
erased, stele-column gripped in sun's tight fist.

THREE

"Where will you spend eternity?"

It is not the question to ask
a middle-aged man who never gets enough
adulation or rough sex, who's never in
the sweet position of wreaking havoc
on those he hates. Not the question
to ask a man with an inconvenient excess
of passion, of imagination.
                                    The pamphlet—
horsefly, sweat-bee—appears under
my windshield wiper at the first I-64 West rest stop
inside Kentucky, and for the next three hours
the Christian question flaps there, teasing
like a Bourbon Street stripper—coy and distant
flashes of what can be seen but never touched.

And so I drive, yearning and murmuring, into heaven
after heaven, past Winchester and Fort Boonesborough,
through Tim McGraw's *Greatest Hits, Volume II*,
while alternative eternities unfurl like morning
glories, azure satin inside my skull.

Here's the Paradise of Domesticity,
                              isolate farmhouse
without neighbors, in the thick of white pine and red oak.
Let John and me sip Scotch and lounge by the fire,
bread rise, beef stew simmer, pear leaves
fill November's windows, bearing the ruddy
textures of mountain dawn. Let there be curled serenities
of cats, the savor of fruits pies without calories,
and an endlessness of unread books.

Here's the Paradise of Justice,
                                    where certain politicians, preachers,
coal-company executives, are mine to disembowel
every blessed morning with this dull hunting knife.
Feed them bread crumbs mixed with coal dust, stained with wine,
and sweet rain water collecting in slurry ponds.
Pin them beneath truckloads of Scripture's overburden,

the broken rock and muck they've made of mountains
and human hope. All heaven's day let rats gnaw
their innards' viscous velvet throbbing, then, like
the vaunted Promethean liver, let their lives grow
back each night, ready to be ripped out on the morrow.

Here's the Paradise of Desire,
                              where every man I want
lies down for me. Let the country boys unpeel
their flannel shirts, pull off their cowboy boots, their
inopportune heterosexuality. Let infinity be black goatees,
armpit musk, thick shoulders aswirl with tattoos. Let timelessness
be bourbon-and-biscuit bellies, beefy pecs dark with fur.
Let Chris, stripped to the waist, roped to a corner chair,
cowboy hat cocked over his eyes, sob gratitude around his bit,
rock and struggle, sweat and drool. Let lean and naked Tim,
all night bound and gagged in bed beside me, rub his broad
back against my chest, nipples harden beneath my fingers
as he tightly rides my slide. Let him rouse sunrise
with kidnapped impatience, ass-grinding ache to be taken again,
fingers fumbling my belly hair, insatiate cloth-muffled moans.

                              Not the question to ask, Christian.
Clearly not the question.
The Tim CD's over. On the last leg
of I-75, wind whips off the pamphlet's
possibilities. Domesticity, justice, desire,
oh, yes, certainly. Here's all we deserve. Here's
76, the exit for Berea. Mist lifts off
the mind-hills. The morning glory, toothless
mouth, collapses into itself. Heaven begs
the question: what then is damned?
Living in fragments while seeing in distance
a clearly conceived whole. It smells
like smoke in here, Room 234 of the Holiday Motel.
I stretch out on the bed wide enough for three,
watch this fancied prism in the window dangle
and turn, splintering today's light into separate selves.

Redneck Food
(for Dorothy Allison
and Erica Abrams Locklear)

Redneck food? Hillbilly vittles?
Call it what you will, sophisticate,
and screw you if your nose is in the air.

Vienna sausages, Lord yes, dipped in
a little yellow mustard, or rat-cheese-
and-fried-baloney sandwiches, mayo-

rich on white bread, or those legendary
forest-wild ramps that make you reek
for days (not true if cooked, but, hell,

anything that will keep the world
at a distance is a precious charm), or,
mmmm, driving back roads with a bag

of fried pork skins and a sweaty bottle
of sweet iced tea, or snapping up country-
ham cat's-head biscuits at the local farmer's

market (said biscuits smothered, on luckiest
Sundays, with sausage gravy spicy with
pepper and onion), or simmering pinto beans

with pork jowl on the back of the stove,
black sorghum atop a steaming slice of
buttered cornbread, collard bowls ham-rich,

dear God! Oh, rough-bearded, wood-musky
redneck brothers, weary-boned mountain
sisters, sit down, dig in, welcome home.

Blue Ridge Heating and Air

He will keep me warm, he will
cool me down, this good-looking cub
from Cambria with his local accent
so like mine, his ruddy goatee
and fine pecs and glutes I make
out despite the baggy jeans
and hoodie. He's in the attic,
in the basement, fooling with
the heat pumps, adding Freon,
calling me "buddy" the way
we mountain men do. He is
today's high-water mark,
among student poems I have
to judge, independent study essays
to read, a bibliography to type up.
So much of life is spent sifting
last year's dead and brittle leaves.
I write a check for services sadly
limited to the mechanical—
the cost of Freon has indeed
gone up. Grinning, he shakes
my hand. Wind-frenzied, pear
petals play like flurries across April's
flower beds, the hyacinths' purple
wounds, last of the species tulips.
God's alms keep us hungry:
a silver hoop in his left earlobe,
stubble on his cheek, and, left
on my desk, his business card.
Tempted as I am to call tonight,
asking if bourbon appeals,
explaining how good a man
of my experience might make him
feel once I had him stripped
and bound to a chair, I will not,
for I have some sense, after nearly
fifty years, of how mean, how

narrow, how ungenerous are
facts. What's left to learn is
how to press palm to palm
and not want more; what's left
to learn is how to be entirely
grateful for what's given,
a handsome boy from Blue Ridge
Heating and Air who made me
hunger one gray spring morning
in my salt-and-pepper forties.

The Misanthrope Contemplates Suburban Development

The bulldozers begin just after dawn—
mud pits, gravel heaps, another pasture gone.

At its edges, the city oozes,
the cheap Sheetrock cubes

of progress. Among the late forest's
sawdust are identical carports, fetal trees,

children cavorting like fleas,
concrete slabbing over

the meadowlark's nest. Who misses
the way wind ripples fields of wheat,

the way satin shivers on a horse's back?
Groundhog's routed out,

gone with nettle and goldenrod.
The cornfield's a golf course.

On the vast asphalt of the mall's
parking lot, cars, adolescent,

rock after dark, rock and rock,
steam and spawn, metastasize.

Night rain's a wild ache for earth.
It pools upon the impermeable,

glistening and reflecting
the dark from which it fell.

Wild

Here it is, the wild—between
decrepit buildings, feathering
up and flowering in empty lots.
What's left, what's original,

thrusts through gaps in concrete.
Queen Anne's lace, red clover probed
by clouds of honeybees, foxtail grass
an emerald iridescence one can't help

but stroke (soft as armpit fur, horse's
chin), and
                    this summer morning's
redneck boy striding shirtless
down Main Street, his torso

today's geometry lesson, his goatee
a virgin hemlock stand (before
the loggers' snarling saws),
his nipples lapped to stipple

by the lust of August zephyrs
(the luckiest tongues
act independent of
any lover's consent), young

back painted with permanence,
smooth-skinned tattoos (flame,
thorn, petal, and vine), here it is,
what's left of wilderness, what's

left of hope, scent of wet black
loam and limestone, curling
and stiffening beneath
his jeans, between his legs.

Here's to the Death of Our Enemies

Memorializing the banal or constructing wish-fulfillment
fantasies, these fill my forties. Men I'd like to rape, men
I'd like to kill. Weight Watchers recipes, cat litter at Walmart,
new varieties of gin. Absurdities yawn between the days
of will-be and might-could. I own several swords,
a scimitar, a dirk. Imagine the neighbors' house charred
down, the barking dogs slashed and brained. Imagine
going entirely berserk, that wildflower honey, that crimson
whipping cream. Right-wingers dead, pious eyes grown black
with flies, heaps and heaps, and our apish executive branch
simmering among them, sweetly gutted. More and more,
manners sleep, fail to fill the breach. The list of hate
grows longer. The skull smokes and churns, a dark ark.
More and more, our Elysium's illegal, our skin is bark.

Gay Redneck, Bloody Tongue

I'm avoiding what I really want—
the barbeque, the grilled pimiento cheese,
the bewitching array of pastries and pies.

Instead, here's the tomato sunburst stuffed
with chicken salad, pink and plump
atop a libidinous bed of fancy lettuce,

served by my favorite waiter, Billy,
sweet and shy country boy with just
the right amount of beer gut

and a wondrously round rump
my inner berserker ogles every
time he turns his back, eminently

edible Billy with his honey-amber beard,
his burly frame a lyric I want to taste
upon my tongue, nip between my teeth,

who shambles over with the check, collects
the empty dolor of my plates, and asks,
"Are you interested in anything else, sir?"

The Old Lecher's DVD Collection

What would the old lecher be
without DVD? Beautiful boys
would pass on the street, shimmer
in the classroom, flex behind
the counter, always clothed,
always distant, entirely
unattainable. But this shining
disc opens the doors to
Paradise, where beauty's always
naked, always fucking.
Whisper the names of the brief
demigods: Logan McCree,
Ricky Sinz, Steve Cruz,
Scott Tanner, et al. Life
without them would diminish
to handshakes, cheek pecks,
stale hugs, the body slowly
becoming a decrepitude
no one can bear to love.
In this audiovisual Eden
nothing's denied save
participation, an eternity
reserved for the voyeur, though
a Tantalean sort of hell
as well, prick perpetually
in hand, always to observe,
never to touch. Still, yes,
proof that passion hasn't entirely
died is well worth the sixty bucks.
Slip it in, push a button, behold!
Praise Eros for this streaming
scene! If you touch it, you stroke
only the glasslike substance
of the video screen, but behind
that, within, in a writhing world
only millimeters beneath your
fingertips, there is euphoric

sound and sight, there's slim
and muscled RJ Danvers,
dark eyebrows and long lashes,
ass and chest curves plastered
with rich dark hair, on his hands
and knees, face contorting
with pain, whimpering
—oh, God could anything be
more thrilling?—"It hurts!"
but Josh West snarls "Take it!"
and only pounds him harder.

Kudzu Jelly

Kudzu sprawls along August's back roads,
clambering over abandoned barns,

smothering the saplings,
lapping like a slow-motion tsunami

at the edges of the porch.
Poor bastard, you must have found

my love much the same, a clinging
morass, mad to consume you, throttling

and tentacled as any obsession.
How I hungered. How you fled.

Twenty-some years later,
I still remember how adorably

you stomped your feet when
you laughed, and the laugh itself,

boyish, I might almost say innocent,
and the intoxicating aromas

of your armpits in late afternoon.
The boy you were and the boy

who loved you so wildly
and so wastefully are dead,

embers buried within
their own gray ash.

And still I manage the odd poem
or two about what a hirsute muse

you were for me. I gather
purple flowers of the kudzu,

distilling pink and perfumed jelly
from an otherwise pestiferous vine.

Gallery, Virginia Tech

She sidesteps pronouns
in her essays mentions
BDSM and pansexuality
in her midsemester journals
dark-haired Goth already
what we Southerners
would call "fine-looking"
her face red her voice
quavering with rage
as she describes for
her fellow students how
little voice or freedom
women in her family have
I want to escort her into
the bright world of
strong Sapphos I know
show her meadows
islands mountains
where women are heard
Instead I show her
websites listing MFA
programs, give her a copy
of Dorothy Allison's
Two or Three Things
I Know for Sure

*

Thank the Goddess
they're still around
these cocky little butch
girls with their flannel
shirts work boots tattoos
softball caps the very breed
of buddy-women who got me
through the aching loneliness
of my youth Braver than

I ever was at that age
Jess sits in the back of
my creative nonfiction class
and reads aloud about
coming out to her mother
Mary shares a sonnet in poetry
workshop about wanting
to marry her lover despite
the backward/devout state
of Virginia and I want to
take them both out for
several pitchers of beer
and barbequed racks
of ribs, later to confess
—despite my leatherbear
penchant for bearded boys
bound down to beds—
my decades-long infatuations
with Jane Seymour
and Jessica Lange

*

Mars and Mercury
let me be the ferocious
father totemic bear
furry and fanged
guardian of the tribe
guiding the young selves
I used to be through
the gauntlet of fire and fear
and jibe Let one prayer
be not selfish and wasted
but selfless and fulfilled

The Gay Redneck Waxes Pugnacious

Ferocious, he thinks, admiring the half-naked man
in the mirror: beefy, hairy chest and belly; tattoos
by the slew; camo shorts, graying goatee; silver torc
harkening back to his warlike ancestors, those scruffy-
wild Celts. *Ah, for a claymore, and the medieval
freedom to destroy.* He flexes both biceps, growls,
and grins. *Brawny berserker! Rebel soldier!
The homophobes I'd slaughter, the invaders I'd slay!*
Stoked up by his own rough-edged looks—*I'd hit that!*—
he swaggers into the kitchen to swill a few burning
mouthfuls of Popcorn Sutton's legal moonshine before
cranking up the soundtrack to *Troy* and commencing
to peel a pound of potatoes for *gratin dauphinois.*

Redneck Roofer

Nothing to be done today but watch his lean
well-inked arms, his torso brown and straining,

sun-golden chest hair a sweaty gleam
above work-filthy pants. He's mesmerizing

this hungry graybeard inside, a lover who moves
from window to window like cats transfixed by the sight

of unreachable birds. Such goateed youth just proves
how little craved is given. Now, from rooftop height,

the godlet descends to earth, to lean against
a maple tree with cell phone, sandwich, and cigarette.

His would-be Daddy's hard, unbeknownst
to this hot, half-naked leaf-shade lounger still musk-wet

from summer's scaffold. As the boy chats with his wife,
one ardor concludes, a sticky waste of life.

A Visit to Pulaski Furniture

I'd transform this scene if I could,
roping not a new sideboard into
the bed of my pickup truck but
this sweet redneck employee of
Pulaski Furniture, who helps me
strong-arm the dark-wood weight.
He's scruffy, the way I prefer
my country boys, sporting a pierced
eyebrow and *Family Guy*'s Stewie
on a sweatshirt. By the time
I return for the second truckload,
a headboard solid enough to
withstand my would-be captive's
roped-up, spread-eagled struggle,
he's sweatily stripped down
to T-shirt and tattered jeans.
I make conversation, asking him
about the Japanese restaurant
across the street, meanwhile
studying the tattoo-swirls that
spill from his sleeves and down
his lightly furred forearms.
Given half a chance, I'd work
his nipples the way I tongue-pit
a black cherry. Instead, we shake
hands. Across his curving torso,
his inadvertent cock-tease of a
T-shirt, the goddamn Pillsbury
Doughboy says, "Hug Me,
Squeeze Me, Take Me Home."

FOUR

The Gay Redneck Gets Highfalutin

No brown beans, chowchow, and cornbread today,
but rather the effete and, to a hillbilly's mind, inexcusably

wasteful British practice of cutting the crusts off bread.
Compulsion having saved the leavings for croutons,

the gay redneck serves dainty cucumber sandwiches
to whimsical female friends who have requested

such a highfalutin experience for their weekend luncheon visit.
As they sip tea brewed in the proper Brown Betty teapot

he has sheepishly christened Polly Prissy-Pants, he picks
tiny remnants of duct tape adhesive from the hair coating

his wrists and shifts uncomfortably on the hard wooden chair,
his hairy ass having been beaten black and blue only last night

by a Skoal-loving brute with a frat paddle, a Fu Manchu,
and a ruthless right arm in the basement den mere yards below

this spread of delicate treaties, Darjeeling, feminine chatter,
and a vase of clumped purple lilacs perfuming the room.

The Misanthrope Grows
Habanero Peppers

"the gold crown/Like a comet streamed fire"
—Robinson Jeffers, *Medea*

Orange-red party hats, a mouth punched in. Scots bonnets, Satan's
change purse, oh God, what possibilities: like renting napalm.
Some use them to heat pots of chili or stew—only one small strip
     will do—

I have more imaginative employments. Word is the Defense
     Department
already coats ship hulls with the juice—what barnacle's brave
     enough
to essay that? I say lift the Pentagon's leg and spray habanero
     essence

on any country who gives us lip, a burnt-orange mist depopulating
the theocratic capitals of the world, dictators combusting down to
mineral gray and flailings. Send these peppers back in time to
     paint

Hitler's moustache, Khomeini's turban, Sherman's underwear.
And oh, the local uses—Jesse Helms, Jerry Falwell acid-basted,
or all those governors in dire need of habanero enemas, the
     gubernatorial

mansions' glass blackening and shattering, lava curling its tongue
down the front steps. And yes, that certain administrator—we all
     have one
in mind—his shirt and tie, eyeballs and bowels anointed with
     something

like Medea's magic, her golden baits to snare the greedy. He's
     rocketing now
for the nearest fountain, a cross between a smudge pot and a
     bowling ball,
a pitch-pine torch trailing dirty smoke, tattered clothes and
     screams.

Come back, you bastard, have another burning bite, another
        medicinal
tablespoon, till your tongue's a battlefield, your mouth a bristle
of javelins. Gargle with jellyfish, sleep with nettles, while

the rest of us praise whatever powers made the magma, the tiger,
and the shark, whatever fallen angel bred such purging heat—
pesticide, emetic, chemical wildfire scorching away the weeds.

Cosmos

My father is eighty-nine.
Bright flowers are what's left

of his garden this late,
mid-October. Color-

blind, I ask: *Lavender?*
Purple? Maroon?

No matter. They are
the last cosmos,

breeze-sway by
torn soil where

half-runners grew.
Bumblebees busy

themselves, supping
in the cups of central

gold. How many years
has he tilled this same

soil, brought in bushels,
filled family shelves

with stored sunlight?
The bees know nothing

of the cold
to come.

They burrow, they
quiver, sunk in

the source
of all delight.

The Old Lecher Does Not Seduce an Overnight Guest

"I go from bedside to bedside, I sleep close
with the other sleepers each in turn."
—Walt Whitman, "The Sleepers"

There are many reasons:
the boy's exactly half my age,
has a partner, albeit long distance,
plus his academic advisor would kill me
if she ever found out, plus he's Southern,
I'm Southern, so, sigh, it's the gentlemanly
thing to do. In fancy only, I stand bold
by the bedside, pull back the covers,
gaze at the long, lithe legs, the thatch
of chest hair. In fancy only, I stuff
a sock in his mouth, haul him up
on hands and knees, kneel behind him,
fumbling with the lube while he nods
and mumbles, impatient, eager mount.
Instead I lie here, just down the hall,
regretful and naked in the fan's caress,
the tabby's insistent loving. I do not touch
myself. Why wake what you cannot feed?
In the morning, he stumbles to the shower
clad only in underwear, a brief parade
of otter-wiry muscle and chestnut fur.
By noon he's biscuit-fed and gone,
continuing to Kentucky, and I'm lying
on the guest bed, already neatly made
by my guest's good country rearing.
I'm pressing to my face the still-moist
towel he used to dry his nakedness, his
every plane and private crevice, looking
for stray beard and body hairs, burrowing
for animal scent. This is what manners
and age have made me—horny cliché,
tally of crimped lusts, lost opportunities.

Rainbow

'So now he knew it had been the tire iron."
—Annie Proulx, "Brokeback Mountain"

1.

I was with them all night long Jack and Ennis   they suffered
I was there on Brokeback Mountain by the fire in the tent
loving in motel beds breathing blood by the Texas highway

I wake early alone my husband far from me in another state
The windows lighten then I rise turn up the heat The furnace
hum is comfort the thickness of brick sword hanging on the wall

2.

Stories waited for me here,
in the state where I was born, region
I remarried, the blue-gray hills
of Southwest Virginia. Tales
like mist rising off mountain roads
after rain, documented or hearsay,
my kind maimed or murdered before my time.
Two women on the Appalachian Trail
and only one survived. He must have seen them
kissing. And the boy's body hikers found
on Brush Mountain, his testicles cut off.

3.

It could have been the stitched rainbow
flag on his backpack that tipped them off.
The orcs grow informed; they learn our codes.
Their SUV missed him by inches, their shouted
"Faggot!" hit him square in the face. You can be
sure that such as they would make kindling
of his bones, given time and happenstance.

4.

Was it that as well, Susanna, a rainbow sticker
on your car, that day you and your wife were driven

off the road, Ford truck full of locals—
mountain men like me, not like me—
howling "Dyke!" I see you shaking
in the ditch along 460, in early spring,
peeper song like shavings of silver,
cress bloom like last flurry in the fields.

5.

A colleague closes my office door, then
whispers it. The kid was straight, yet
he was beaten so badly that now he bears
a metal plate inside his head. His hat
"was too gay." What I'm seeing is hot pink,
or orange, colors of plumeria, a clump
of Victorian violets. Not the sort of hat
I wear: dun baseball caps, cowboy hats
in black and brown. The dull colors
of moths, evolving to adapt to industrial
smoke. I am still whole, undamaged,
still able to write these words today.

6.

My husband, who was not there, swears
they were simply drunk. All I know is
my last night in that rental after eight years,
3 am, student party on the porch across the street,
sweet night in May, new leaves' gold-green,
and the *thunk thunk* that woke me, stones lobbed
against my mailbox one by one. All I know is
I wanted to cower in the house or call
the cops. But pride pulled on my jeans,
T-shirt, cowboy boots, black drover and
baseball cap, and hate slipped the scimitar
down the coat's inside pocket. Aragorn's elven
hunting knife, *Lord of the Rings* collectible,
etched with Elvish, "Foe of Morgoth's Realm,"
easier to conceal than my Scottish dirk or
Nordic sword, and twice as sharp. Oh,
the hostess saw me coming, the "Sorry,
Sorry" started, the lame denials, and so
the crowd dispersed. I turned, tensing,

waiting for a stone upside the head, between
my shoulder blades. I sat on my porch, pulled
out the knife, and, God, the heft of it felt finer
than love. I thumb-stroked the blade's edge,
I watched their cars one by one depart.
I stalked the yard's edge like a snuffling wolf,
pushed my face into honeysuckle bloom,
studied the heap of stones scattered about
the mailbox, across the front steps, sure
proof I was not dreaming. All I know is
any foe who came after me I would have
sliced with that knife fated instead to spend
what little left there was of that spring
night at arm's reach beside my bed.

7.

Jo raised me well, the woman who led me out.
I heard of bar raids, cops with rubber hoses
that beat but do not bruise. I learned to look
for back doors in any gay club just in case
quick escape proved needful.

Along with country-music beauties
Chris Cagle, Toby Keith, Tim McGraw,
handsome captives to keep me company
in my 4X4 on long back-road drives—
their voices lap my ears, I lick the lyrics
of their chest hair and sweet goatees—
there's the black-handled hunting knife
Jo gave me thirty years ago, kept hidden
beneath my seat. Case XX, it has whittled
no flesh, no bone, only twigs and twine.
It could stand some sharpening.

8.

The meetings, the meetings, the talk
of community principles, campus climate, and meanwhile

in Richmond they try to pass more laws
against us, and meanwhile a kid caught sleeping with his boyfriend

has the whole dorm floor roused against him
and next morning must move out, and what I want, I must

admit, is something like animal skin nailed
in warning to shed doors out back, which is, I here explain to those
        urbane,

what country people do to predators, not unlike
the heads that used to rot on pikes along the walls of London's Tower,

and meanwhile, after the meetings, the meetings,
the talk, the talk, my student Chet insists someone here will have to
        die—

martyred beneath swung pipe or tire iron, left in ditch
or dumpster—to split this black chrysalis, to save this state's soul.

9.

I was with them again all night long Jack and Ennis
then woke this drizzly Christmas Day safe beside John
We drive to my hometown where three generations share

a country family feast Scalloped potatoes deviled eggs
home-baked bread and ham butternut squash pie Sated
I step out well-warmed with bourbon stand in cold rain

wishing for a world revised only mountains and my kin
my kind Above Hinton sheer slopes white loom of cove-fog
This is the place to live in beauty and to die

Sudden sun-scatter and now a rainbow arcs its bridge
across the valley astride the town Nothing we can climb
as yet but still I tip my cowboy hat and watch until it wanes

Country Boys, Elkins

"...he will become a lover of all physical beauty,
and will relax the intensity of his passion for one
particular person..."—Plato, *The Symposium*

You're welcome to the rest of it: urban chaff,
New York, San Francisco, LA, the latest
spiky-haired, smooth-chested emaciate posing
in—fuck, I don't know jackshit about fashion—
Armani, Gucci?—in the slick pages of *Out*.
The well-groomed city twinks, take 'em all,
every last effete cologne-reeking one. Give me
any hill-girt hamlet—for instance today's
Elkins, West Virginia, much like the railroad
town where I grew up, where I first developed
such redneck aesthetics—give me country boys.

Plato was right. I loved and I loved and
I loved and I loved, one brawny rural brute
after another, decade after decade, till
my devotion honed and evolved. Here's
Beauty, the Ideal Form of the Mountain Man
manifesting through these hot young hillbillies
glowing inside today's Ramps and Rails Fest.
Men with scuffed cowboy boots, scruffy beards,
chest hair curling over tank top collars,
dirty baseball caps sporting the Stars and Bars.
Chunky chests, chunky bellies, born of beer
and doughnuts, baloney sandwiches, fried
pork skins. Big arms streaked with tattoos,
lean arms sinewy with hard work's muscle,
they're all versions of my youth, as if, loving
them, I might learn to love the world, and later,
most difficult of all, learn to love myself.
Twilight, they will bounce down back roads
in their trucks, listening to Brad Paisley, Toby Keith,
Tim McGraw, heading home to women, brats,
a cozy couch, a cheap six-pack (a few like me

snuggling with burly husbands), but right now
they're striding around Elkins' town square,
dense and hairy, flexing and smiling in late April
sun, armpits leaving sweet trails of musk. Here's
the warrior-god I've worshipped, emulated
all my life, with a wavy auburn goatee, big forearms
glistening with fur. He's Wordsworth's Man of Nature,
Voltaire's Noble Savage, handing me a ramp eggroll—
There ya go, buddy!—impish grin like Sylvanus
or Pan, this gleaming moment's rustic deity.

Hemlocks

A tiny insect,
    the woolly adelgid,
        is eating the needles.

Without boughs
    to sough, the wind
        has less and less to say.

The green dwindles,
    twigs brittle and brown,
        like black beards gone silver,

the wilderness
    leaching away.
        Inside spheres of hemlock

shade, your body turns
    to emerald. Jewels
        are shattered one by one,

the abacus of age
    tallying the black
        numerals, tallying.

Unframed by limbs,
    the vistas disappear.
        No composition now,

only stumps and vacant air.
    The forest shrivels,
        the graveyard fills.

Chestnut, hemlock, ivorybill,
    cancer, gallstone, adelgid.
        Emptied out,

my aunt's cornfield,
    my grandmother's house,
        my mother's clothes.

Making Love to Granite

He's mere water and mineral, I know,
for I once sifted the gray-white silt spilled
from cardboard box into funerary urn,

but I am fascinated nevertheless—the usual
queer desire veiled beneath hearty butch
country manners—watching him, sweet

warmth of the animate, as he shifts granite
samples so my husband and I might choose
a color for kitchen countertops to come.

I can't quite recall when I last had
such a strong ache to kiss, to embrace
a man I hardly know—it's a heaviness

hard to resist, obdurate as the weight
of racked granite slabs, how they yearn,
how they want to fall, give into landscape's

lodestone pull, lie flat along the grassy
body of the earth—but of course
he's married, a father, etc., ho hum,

and my husband's right here, so I resist,
remembering nevertheless exactly
the same transfixed and unwise

leaning, when, once, an undergrad
cozily drugged during wisdom-teeth
extraction, I stared up at the handsome

oral surgeon and almost pulled him down
on top of me, though even that drunk
thought better of it, what with all

the damned nurses around. Thirty years
later, and here's the same longing, good
for nothing but poems and jack-off fantasies.

Beneath today's layered T-shirts (his nipples
must be stiff in this February chill),
his hidden muscles move as he heaves

great sheets of stone. His litany
of seduction's spoken—*Luna Pearl, Tuscany
Brown, Caledonia, Black Galaxy*. Mine's

silently memorized for want of a camera—
about five foot nine, the size my caveman
would hoist over his shoulder, goatee

the hue of clover honey, a great grin,
what my grandmother would have called
butter teeth, the brown skin and early wrinkles

about the brow and eyes that men earn
who work outdoors. Igneous texture
of the living, yes, Lord, as rippled

and as rich as these polished quartz
glitters inside the Crema Bordeaux
we settle on. With a rubber hammer,

he knocks off a remnant shard, hands me
what solid I can take home. Within the winter
sun, his hand grips mine, a *Thanks-and-bye-*

buddy shake that lasts three seconds, heat
far too fast to savor. We're done, he's done,
broad shoulders and small butt sucked

down the vortex of the vanishing point.
Now it's fried pork chop sandwiches
at Snappy Lunch and then the drive north,

climbing Virginia's steeps to Fancy Gap.
The forest dells are shaded laurel-
thick, the icefalls gray glass, crystal

of temple columns, frozen finger-joints
the fate of March is soon to thaw.
Some stone's temporary. My biceps

would be dense as flesh can be, lifting
him into my arms. The granite chunk
in my hands refuses to warm, though

I stroke it and stroke it, stroke how
he might look naked, in a pool of morning
light, along his belly's crest the lyric

scroll of honey-colored hair. How did
years of fire end here, quartz no touch
can melt, winter's grave lump in my lap?

John's Garden

I speak of it only now, as it withers.
Speech as celebration, I barely remember that.

Speech as scar tissue, that makes more sense.
Autumn's a whirlpool, a narrowing. We're almost

to the end of it. As are the anemones you planted,
and the lavender, and the morning glories I admire,

chill days in the driveway, sapphire like
those that twined my grandmother's porch,

with white pentacles for throats, gold-dust
stamens, texture like a young man's skin.

Shriveling, the grape tomatoes, the chives and basil.
Once, in anger, you swore you'd become nothing

but my housekeeper. True, touch grows sparse.
My retort: I'm erstwhile stud become cook

and laundress. When did we lose
the gift of praise? Disheartened gardener,

every morning I'm standing in sad delight
before the grieving supernovae of sunflowers,

caressing their petals as I would a lover about to
leave. Would I be more passionate, more giving,

if I were dying, if you were dying, or dramatically
about to decamp with some young, erratic, hugely hung

musician? We're dying fast enough. Promise to be
here next year, to plant the garden of my mornings,

the garden of the sun. I'll do my best to be kind, though
beauty is, I fear, after all these years, beyond me,

as is fascination. Our descent's a slow, gentle
grade, a common fate. Epithalamia

lack the conflict I crave, the epic and addictive extremes
of love lost or unrequited. The elegiac tone's my talent.

Not my muse? Count your blessings. You're earth,
I'm fire. I would say, extending the metaphor, you're root

and I'm flower, but that seems vain, even for me. Love's either/
or: poetry or longevity. Our years have chosen the latter.

High Life
(for Scott Goebel)

I'm wondering what the devout
Presbyterian founders of Maryville
College would think of this, a big
mountaineer getting gently stewed,
to use the Mencken phrase, here
in front of Thaw Hall, fittingly
named, for my buddy Scott with
the amazing blue eyes has left
the back of his pickup truck open
and kindly invited me to help myself
to his cooler of Miller High Life
while he attends the next session
of the Appalachian Studies Conference.
I'm used to stronger stuff, bourbon
or gin, so I've got to blame the too-busy-
to-have-lunch growly belly that has me
buzzed so fast in this devoutly dry
campus where I sip from my huggie
when no one's looking. I'm guessing
no one's guessing that the big bearded
redneck in faded jeans, black leather vest,
and black cowboy boots who's sprawled
on the tailgate, black straw Resistol
tilted over his eyes, is hotly eying
young men behind those dark glasses,
but so I am, the sun palms my neck
like a kingly lover, the beech trees
are brandishing new buds among
the papery poverty of last year's leaves,
the redbuds and crab apples are hum-
ming bee-busy purple and fragile pink,
and here comes a hot little guy with
a brown goatee and a buzz cut, big
pecs shoving out the front of his tight
gray T-shirt, and today, in this particular
state of drunkenness, for once it's

enough to look but not touch, though
usually I wax surly studying such
delectable prey, law and conscience
being tiresome heavy hands interfering
perpetually with my perpetually porno-
graphic abduction fantasies. No, today,
reality's for a few seconds sufficient.
This is the high life, simply lounging here,
recalling how Miss Dolly gives Billy Ray
the eye in a mid-90s CMT music video
and says, *I'm old enough to be that boy's
lover,* a sentiment I can only echo as,
innocently unaware of my politely caged
appetite, this college kid strolls past me,
a bearded boy so beautiful I forgive him
for not begging me to take him home,
so beautiful I briefly forgive the world,
finish my beer in salute, pop open another.

Sleeping in a Tim McGraw T-Shirt

is, of course, as close as you can get. You're naked otherwise,
here beneath the flannel sheets of southwest Virginia

married middle age. Your favorite star is far remote,
with wife and children on their huge farm outside Nashville, or

on the road again for another concert tour, or
in the studio perfecting his plangent country twang. And he is

here, your ideal bondage bottom: dark eyes,
black-straw Resistol, fine lips framed by brown beard,

half-open shirt displaying thick chest hair, torso pressed warm
against yours, hands roped behind his back. Your husband

shifts away snoring, and you are sleepless yet again.
Too much gin. Embrace yourself, embrace Tim.

Cowboy, Bad Boy, Real Good Man.
Everything distant you have ever desired.

That's his rapt heart beating against yours.
That's his tight submission, your right fist's sweaty grip.

The Gay Redneck, Hankering After Celebrities, Hikes the New River Trail

The outfit's *Brokeback* to match the aching spine—
the sort of rawhide jacket and felt cowboy hat
Ennis Del Mar might have worn—which leads me
to memories of Jake Gyllenhaal naked, on his knees,
grunting with invaded discomfort in a high
mountain tent, and that at least makes my sacro-
iliac joint feel a little better. That, and my cautious
loping along this woodland rail-to-trail, my compulsive
autumnal botanizing: pokeberries, samaras of ash
and box elder, dying wingweed, fallen mulberry leaves,
the scattered seeds of tulip trees. This blessedly far
from human beings, little sounds save the occasional
crow or woodpecker, and, in my head, the latest
truck-cab tune, Thomas Rhett's "It Goes Like This,"
his furry chest, black beard and sloppy bangs almost
worth the complications and consequences of
a kidnapping. Boys so beautiful should always be
bruised and sore in all the right places, as I find myself
today, despite my distance from cities, backed-up traffic,
condo sprawl and suburban malls, the fascinatingly
fashionable Gay Community. Thanks to ornery
defiance, appetite, and a lot of luck, I have found
in my native mountains everything I need, and so
let me take this opportunity to congratulate myself
on having the damn-fine good sense to stay.

Gold

An altered look, said Dickinson.
Yes. As if morning mist

were green-gold,
or rainclouds

were chartreuse,
new leaf clinging to April

and Appalachia's
dark, long-bare limbs.

Again and again,
the earth regains its youth.

Twenty years
have gleamed and grayed

since the spring
we shared.

The color of these hills
captures that mislaid morning

in a distant city,
sleeping together

for the first time, naked,
side by side.

I woke before you,
pulled back the veil covering your body,

and stared in wonder
at your repose, the hard

and helpless muscles
of your arms, the brown hair

mossing your chest, your unconscious
cock, your breath's rise and fall.

Our beards were still glossy and dark,
though even then my hair was thinning.

There was hope for us, I thought.
If I loved you hard enough

you would leave him and choose to stay
with me. So I watched you sleep,

aching
to touch you, to top you,

but terrified,
for then you might wake

into distance and defense.
You were my son

then, my only child.
Once, however briefly,

this tenderness had a home,
and all my bonfire

passion was welcomed, not wasted.
I was right, I was right

in my suspicion, that when you woke,
all springs would leave with you,

and every April after
would be word, not flesh,

and I would hold nothing
so young and golden again.

At Starr Hill Brewery, The Old Lecher Drinks Love Deep
(for Sarah)

The tasting room bartender's Buck. Married of course,
with the sort of looks still capable of making me ache:
close brown beard, hazel eyes, full lips, sweet curves
of pecs and ass beneath T-shirt and shorts. I'm smitten,
as in *smite/smote/smitten*, struck with something strong
and stunning like a sword or club. He's full of cub-smiles,
long-lashed glances, soft Piedmont accent, ready to serve
us the brewery's offerings: red ale, lager, IPA, a German
Hefeweizen called, with God's usual vicious humor,
The Love. *Yeah, yeah, boy, tap your Daddy some love*,
so I want to growl. Instead, to Sarah, I whisper,
I want him for Christmas, and, while I'm entirely
tongue-tied around a boy this luscious, God love
her Viking maiden looks and bubblicious breasts,
Sarah strikes up a conversation, so that he'll move
closer, so this shy old grizzly might talk to him. Midlife
cliché: I'm fifty, this boy's not yet thirty, I've become
my father, yes, now, how well I understand that foul
affair with the much younger secretary, I've become
that sort of man in that sort of marriage—comfortable,
static, breeding like bacteria these pathetic, unseemly
longings. Marital passion's very much a part of the past,
martinis a less-than-lucid substitute for affection, plus,
dumb hillbilly, I've stubbornly insisted on remaining
in my native hills, where boys who might reciprocate
my lusts are few and far between. *There's no fool like
an old fool*, as my mother used to say, yes, shit, fuck,
sadly true, thirteen years coupled and I've ended
where I'd begun, only wanting men I can't have.
This boy's here to prove to me that I ain't quite
dead yet, that, given the right circumstances,
the almost unimaginable miracle of mutuality,
I'm still capable of depth, delight, pure foolishness,
but of course Buck knows none of this, my soft
panting barely repressed by good Southern manners—

these dreams of seeing him naked, nuzzling his furry
crevices, roughly roping and gagging and riding him,
the obsessive, repetitive, and endlessly fascinating
whirlpool of fetish. Probability has never been
accommodating, even in my satyritic youth, and today's
futile hankering's further proof that possibilities
are fast dwindling down to a vanishing point, that spot
on the horizon where the interstate's swallowed
like a votive's last millimeter of wick. Coming soon,
the age all long-lived lechers achieve, when the only
friendly prick's one's own and that only if the limp
brute agrees to work. God, isn't this tiresome? *Buck,*
sweet cub, time for the cuffs; spread your furry
thighs and gnaw this gag while I eat your hole,
then take you up the ass. See how delightful fiction
is set cheek-by-jowl beside tedious truth? Well, enough
of horny fantasies and whinging geezer-complaint.
A Starr Hill little growler's my glassy souvenir, so as
to remember the sweet way that desire, however
unsatisfied, made luminous one summer afternoon.
I have my cub fill it to the brim with his love, a liquid
strong and foamy Sarah and I might suck on as we wend
the windy green back roads of Albemarle County.

Gay Redneck, with Baby Stroller

Mid-October weekend, back in his hometown
of Hinton, West Virginia, for the Railroad Days
street fair, he's threading the swarm of leaf-peeper
city folks just off the train, catching up with family,
admiring a few hot bearded boys in dirty camo,
and gobbling in rapid succession two hot dogs,
slaw-topped barbeque, and one country ham
sandwich. "You look like a West Virginian!"
says his classy cousin, in from the Bluegrass State,
in reference to his Justin boots, Western drover,
Shady Brady cowboy hat, *Hill Billy* T-shirt, bushy
gray goatee grown down to his breastbone.
"I am!" he says, flexing an arm and tipping his hat.
While his sister slips into a produce market
to fetch tomatoes, rat cheese, and creecy greens,
he stands by her baby stroller and watches over
his nephew while he sleeps. The two no doubt
look like just another redneck daddy and his son,
living the safety and the ease of those born
normal, those with less to hate and less to fear,
an existence he can barely imagine, only
thirty years and a block away from the spot
where Shorty Bennett called him *Queer*, stopped
the truck, strode over, and punched him in the face.

Training The Enemy

"America I'm putting my queer shoulder to the wheel"
—Allen Ginsberg

Well, Appalachia, you've done it.
You've made a man of me. I'm no longer that
shy, bespectacled boy who aroused contempt
in the sternest of you, the boy who lived for
Tolkien's Middle Earth and Mary Renault's Greece,
The X-Men, *The Avengers*, *Bonanza*, and other
alternatives more appealing and heroic than
Hinton, West Virginia. Oh, I was timid, I was
polite, the sort of little gentleman my mother
wanted me to be, fit for dinner parties or idle
chat in candlelit antebellum drawing rooms.
Elderly ladies doted on me; I flattered their
twinkling arabesque brooches, their rose bushes'
hot pink. Not effeminate really, just unsure,
awkward, amorphous, sexless, another pudgy
adolescent who learned early he was no good,
nothing special at sports, and so pumped out
A's for want of more manly achievements.

Your mockery, Appalachia, made me
change. One fist upside my mouth made me
cut off high school's long hippie hair, wear
lumberjack boots and leather jackets, lift
weights. My hometown would not know me
now, my shaved head and silvered beard, furry
hard pecs, cowboy hats, tattoos, boots, rage.
Watch me shoot the redneck shit as well
as any local, puffing stogies and sipping bourbon
straight. What I read's martial, new translations
of *The Iliad*, *Beowulf*, *The Saga of the Volsungs*.
What I collect's dirks, scimitars, swords.
How's that for manly? Now do you approve?
Hell, nothing's changed except how much I hate.
Yesterday a slim queer kid told me how

half his dorm floor turned on him, how he had
to move out or bleed. America, Appalachia, my sweet
small mountain towns, I'm native here, I'm going
nowhere. It's a damn fool who makes a youth suffer,
makes a child feel wrong, then teaches that new-
honed foe how to grow tough, how to grow strong.

Redneck Bouquet
(for John)

A mason jar
of blooming thistles

on the mantelpiece,
the same belligerent blossom

inked into my left forearm.
Scotland's echo,

Nemo me inpune lacessit,
or, in Scots, *Wha daur meddle*

wi me? or, in hillbilly,
Nobody fucks with me

and gets away with it.
Nearly every inch a thorn

or prick, guarding
that lavender bloom

soft as duckling feathers,
as a man's glans, hair-

rimmed areola or musky
nether gate.

Scent of summer meadows,
of the sweaty hayfields,

savagery brandishing
a sword, born to shield

what is beloved, what is tender.
Stick your rules up your ass,

is its snarled language.
Don't get too close.

I will live as I please.
I will grow where

it is isolate and free,
far from groomed lawns,

in the rebels' lofty bastions,
in the outlaws' waste places.

ACKNOWLEDGMENTS

Many thanks to the editors of the following journals and anthologies, in which many of these poems first appeared.

Chelsea Station: "Trounced by Princess Puppy: On the Difficulties of Being a Gay Writer in Appalachia," "The Gay Redneck Rationalizes Pie Day," "Storm Windows," "Harland Sanders Café and Museum," "The Old Lecher's DVD Collection," and "Redneck Bouquet"

Impossible Archetype: "The Gay Redneck Devours Draper Mercantile," "Green Man," "Krispy Kreme Fantasia," "Joe-Pye Weed," "John's Garden," and "Rainbow Chard, Bear Bouquet"

LGBTQ Fiction and Poetry from Appalachia, edited by Jeff Mann and Julia Watts: "The Gay Redneck Devours Draper Mercantile," "Yellow-Eye Beans," and "Training the Enemy"

Pine Mountain Sand and Gravel: Contemporary Appalachian Writing: "Buzzard," "Pressure-Washer Prayer," "The Misanthrope Contemplates Suburban Development," "Kudzu Jelly," "The Misanthrope Grows Habanero Peppers," "Training the Enemy," and "Cosmos"

Quarried: Three Decades of Pine Mountain Sand and Gravel, edited by Richard Hague: "Kudzu Jelly" and "The Misanthrope Grows Habanero Peppers"

Appalachian Heritage: "Yellow-Eye Beans," "Daddy's Cabbage," and "Hemlocks"

Journal of Appalachian Studies: "Yellow-Eye Beans" and "Rainbow" (included in the essay "Risk, Religion, and Invisibility")

Glitterwolf Magazine: "The Gay Redneck Visits Heavener Hardware" and "Redneck Roofer"

Hamilton Stone Review: "Almost Heaven"

The Queer South: LGBTQ Writers on the American South, edited by Douglas Ray: "Dear Pastor Dickweed" and "Blue Ridge Heating and Air"

Off the Rocks: "Huntington Lane"

This Assignment Is So Gay: LGBTIQ Poets on the Art of Teaching, edited by Megan Volpert: "Country Kids" and "Gallery, Virginia Tech"

Vinyl Poetry: "The Mountaineer Queer, Diagnosed as Dying, Runs Amok"

Electric Dirt: "The Gay Redneck Invites City Sappho for a Rural Visit"

ImageOutWrite: "Mike"

Anthology of Appalachian Writers: "The Misanthrope Visits Eggleston, Virginia"

The James White Review: "Crickets"

Hard Lines: Rough South Poetry, edited by Daniel Cross Turner and William Wright: "A Brief Christian Visit"

Velvet Mafia: Dangerous Queer Fiction: "Here's to Fucking the Famous"

The Black Napkin: "Where Will You Spend Eternity?"

Ganymede Unfinished, edited by Bryan Borland: "Wild" and "A Visit to Pulaski Furniture"

Knockout: "Here's to the Death of Our Enemies"

A Gay and Gray Anthology, edited by Cookie Crumbles, Randy Gresham, and Marc Frazier: "The Old Lecher Does Not Seduce an Overnight Guest"

Hibernation and Other Poems by Bear Bards, edited by Ron J. Suresha: "Country Boys, Elkins," "Making Love to Granite," "Gold," and "At Starr Hill Brewery, the Old Lecher Drinks Love Deep"

Nin: "Sleeping in a Tim McGraw T-shirt"

Lovejets: Queer Male Poets on 200 Years of Walt Whitman, edited by Raymond Luczak: "Training the Enemy"

The Sanguine Woods: "Redneck Bouquet"

ABOUT THE AUTHOR

Jeff Mann grew up in Covington, Virginia, and Hinton, West Virginia, receiving degrees in English and forestry from West Virginia University. His poetry, fiction, and essays have appeared in numerous publications and earned him such acclaim as two Lambda Literary Awards, the Pauline Réage Novel Award, the John Preston Short Fiction Award, and the Saints and Sinners Literary Festival Hall of Fame. His work was included in the first Official Literary Map of West Virginia, unveiled at the West Virginia Book Festival. He teaches creative writing at Virginia Tech in Blacksburg, Virginia.

THANK YOU

Many thanks to Steve Berman and Ryan Vance for creating a handsome book.

Thanks to Jakk Blood for once more being a cover-cub.

Thanks to L.S. King for the photographs.